D0777136

A PERSPECTIVES FLIP BOOK

The Split History of the
WOMEN'S SUFFRAGE MOVEMENT

SUFFRAGISTS' PERSPECTIVE

BY DON NARDO

CONTENT CONSULTANT:
Zoe Burkholder, PhD
Assistant Professor, College of Education and Human Services
Montclair State University

COMPASS POINT BOOKS
a capstone imprint

Compass Point Books are published by Capstone,
1710 Roe Crest Drive, North Mankato, Minnesota 56003
www.capstonepub.com

LIBRARY OF CONGRESS CATALOGING-IN-PUBLICATION DATA

Nardo, Don, 1947-
  The split history of the women's suffrage movement / by Don Nardo.
    pages cm. – (Compass point books. Perspectives flip books)
  Includes bibliographical references and index.
  Summary: "Describes the opposing viewpoints of women's suffragists and anti-suffragists in the
United States beginning in the mid-19th century"—Provided by publisher.
  ISBN 978-0-7565-4735-6 (library binding)
  ISBN 978-0-7565-4791-2 (paperback)
  ISBN 978-0-7565-4797-4 (eBook PDF)
  1. Women—Suffrage—United States—Juvenile literature. 1. Title.
  JK1898.N36 2014
  324.6'230973—dc23   2013034817

EDITOR
BRENDA HAUGEN

LIBRARY CONSULTANT
KATHLEEN BAXTER

DESIGNER
ASHLEE SUKER

PRODUCTION SPECIALIST
LAURA MANTHE

MEDIA RESEARCHER
WANDA WINCH

IMAGE CREDITS

Suffragists' Perspective:
Art Resource, N.Y.: National Portrait Gallery/Smithsonian Institution, 7; Corbis: Bettmann, 5,
26; Library of Congress, 8, Prints and Photographs Division, cover (all), 12, 14, 15, 16, 18, 19,
20, 23, 25, 28, 29

Anti-Suffragists' Perspective:
Bryn Mawr College Library: C.C.Catt Albums, 19; Corbis: Bettmann, 6; Getty Images: Topical
Press Agency, 25; The Granger Collection, NYC, 5; Library of Congress: Prints and Photographs
Division, cover (all), 11, 15, 16, 21, 26, 29, Rare Book and Special Collections Division, 22;
Timothy Hughes Rare & Early Newspapers, 13

Printed in the United States of America in Stevens Point, Wisconsin.
092013   007767WZS14

Table of
Contents

THE SMART, COURAGEOUS WOMEN

*E*arly in July 1848, an ad in an issue of a small upstate New York newspaper stated:

> A convention to discuss the social, civil, and religious rights of women
>
> will be held in the Wesleyan Chapel, Seneca Falls, New York,
>
> on Wednesday and Thursday, the 19th and 20th of July current;
>
> commencing at 10 a.m. During the first day the meeting will be held
>
> exclusively for women, who are earnestly invited to attend. The public
>
> generally are invited to be present on the second day.

Elizabeth Cady Stanton speaks at the Seneca Falls convention.

The meeting, attended by fewer than 300 people, marked the beginning of the women's rights movement in the United States. These early social reformers demanded civil rights for women. Chief among the rights was suffrage—the right to vote. At the time no major nation in the world allowed female suffrage.

There had been a few minor exceptions in the past. The Corsican Republic, which controlled the Mediterranean island of Corsica from 1755 to 1769, allowed women's suffrage. Also, at least one woman in the original 13 British American colonies actually voted. Her name was Lydia Taft. Because she was wealthy and influential in the town of Uxbridge, Massachusetts, she was allowed to vote in town meetings. In addition, between the years 1776 and 1807 the state of New Jersey allowed women who owned a certain amount of property to vote.

Such examples remained odd historical exceptions to a general rule in the vast majority of societies. It held that women were second-class citizens. They could neither vote nor run for public office. The main reason was that most people in those days simply accepted what they saw as gender norms. The common belief was that women were weak, incapable of complex thought, and ruled by their emotions.

In contrast, men were generally viewed as strong, complex thinkers, and in control of their emotions. It seemed logical, therefore, that men were better suited to hold down jobs and be in charge of politics. And as members of the perceived weaker, less capable gender, women were expected to run the home, raise the children, and support their husbands' political views and personal dreams.

EDUCATED, PASSIONATE PEOPLE

The first major, organized attempt to change the situation in the United States was spearheaded by two smart, energetic, and courageous women. One was Lucretia Mott, who as a young woman had taught school in what is now Millbrook, New York. German-born social reformer Carl Schurz met Mott when she was 61. He later described her in these words: "I thought her the most beautiful old lady I had ever seen. Her features were of exquisite fineness. Not one of the wrinkles with which age had marked her face, would one have wished away. Her dark eyes beamed with intelligence."

The other early founder of the U.S. women's movement was Elizabeth Cady Stanton. A devoted mother and social reformer,

Lucretia Mott was a social reformer who also opposed slavery.

she lived in Seneca Falls, New York. "The wearied, anxious look of the majority of women," she later wrote, "impressed me with a strong feeling that some active measures should be taken to remedy the wrongs of society in general, and of women in particular."

Elizabeth Stanton and Lucretia Mott first met in 1840. At the time they were attending the World Anti-Slavery Convention in London, England. There they found themselves surrounded by educated, passionate people like themselves. Stanton and Mott talked about putting together the same kind of gathering for women's rights.

Like many other women of their day, especially educated ones, Stanton and Mott felt that it was unfair that women had fewer rights than men. It was particularly upsetting that women could not vote or hold public office. Yet they did not desire these rights simply to gain political power. They saw the right to vote as a means to other ends as well. With more political power, women could more easily inherit property, for instance. They could also have a better chance of gaining custody of their children in a divorce. At the time men were awarded custody more often. The women also believed they could improve women's access to higher education. Most college graduates then were men.

For Stanton and Mott, the opportunity to organize a meeting to address these issues came eight years later. During the early summer of 1848, they and three other like-minded New York women agreed to hold a convention in July. To publicize it, they placed an ad in the *Seneca County Courier*.

Our Roll of Honor

Containing all the
Signatures to the "Declaration of Sentiments"
Set Forth by the First

Woman's Rights Convention,

held at
Seneca Falls, New York
July 19-20, 1848

LADIES:

Lucretia Mott	Sophronia Taylor	Rachel D. Bonnel
Harriet Cady Eaton	Cynthia Davis	Betsey Tewksbury
Margaret Pryor	Hannah Plant	Rhoda Palmer
Elizabeth Cady Stanton	Lucy Jones	Margaret Jenkins
Eunice Newton Foote	Sarah Whitney	Cynthia Fuller
Mary Ann M'Clintock	Mary H. Hallowell	Mary Martin
Margaret Schooley	Elizabeth Conklin	P. A. Culvert
Martha C. Wright	Sally Pitcher	Susan R. Doty
Jane C. Hunt	Mary Conklin	Rebecca Race
Amy Post	Susan Quinn	Sarah A. Mosher
Catherine F. Stebbins	Mary S. Mirror	Mary E. Vail
Mary Ann Frink	Phebe King	Lucy Spalding
Lydia Mount	Julia Ann Drake	Lovina Latham
Delia Mathews	Charlotte Woodward	Sarah Smith
Catherine C. Paine	Martha Underhill	Eliza Martin
Elizabeth W. M'Clintock	Dorothy Mathews	Maria E. Wilbur
Malvina Seymour	Eunice Barker	Elizabeth D. Smith
Phebe Mosher	Sarah R. Woods	Caroline Barker
Catherine Shaw	Lydia Gild	Ann Porter
Deborah Scott	Sarah Hoffman	Experience Gibbs
Sarah Hallowell	Elizabeth Leslie	Antoinette E. Segur
Mary M'Clintock	Martha Ridley	Hannah J. Latham
Mary Gilbert		Sarah Sisson

GENTLEMEN:

Richard P. Hunt	William S. Dell	Nathan J. Milliken
Samuel D. Tillman	James Mott	S. E. Woodworth
Justin Williams	William Burroughs	Edward F. Underhill
Elisha Foote	Robert Smallbridge	George W. Pryor
Frederick Douglass	Jacob Mathews	Joel Bunker
Henry W. Seymour	Charles L. Hoskins	Isaac VanTassel
Henry Seymour	Thomas M'Clintock	Thomas Dell
David Spalding	Saron Phillips	E. W. Capron
William G. Barker	Jacob P. Chamberlain	Stephen Shear
Elias J. Doty	Jonathan Metcalf	Henry Hatley
John Jones		Azaliah Schooley

A roll of honor listed all those who signed the Declaration of Sentiments at the Seneca Falls convention in 1848.

ALL MEN AND WOMEN EQUAL?

The conference went even better than the organizers had hoped. About 250 women arrived on the first day. And even though the newspaper ad had called for attendance by women only that day, about 40 men unexpectedly showed up as well. One was the famous African-American social reformer Frederick Douglass. Mott, Stanton, and the other organizers happily welcomed the male attendees.

The event consisted mostly of speeches and discussions. Stanton gave one of the most moving speeches. The time had come, she declared, "for the question of women's wrongs to be laid before the public." The issue of woman's rights was of utmost importance, she stated. Furthermore, she and the others present "dare assert that woman stands by the side of man—his equal."

Stanton also penned the meeting's official written statement. Titled the "Declaration of Sentiments and Resolutions," it was purposely done in the format and style of the U.S. Declaration of Independence. One section of Stanton's version stated: "We hold these truths to be self-evident: that all men and women are created equal; that they are endowed by their Creator with certain inalienable rights; that among these are life, liberty, and the pursuit of happiness."

Among the most crucial rights women should have, the declaration said, was the right to vote. Existing governments, it continued, held what amounted to a tyranny over women. Because women could not vote, they had no say in choosing their leaders.

SCORN AND ABUSE

The right to vote was not the only women's issue that Elizabeth Cady Stanton fought for. She was also a tireless champion of female equality with men in employment, income, and custody of children in divorces. In a speech delivered in 1848, she pointed out: "Every allusion to the degraded and inferior position occupied by woman all over the world, has ever been met by scorn and abuse. From the man of highest mental cultivation, to the most degraded wretch who staggers in the streets do we hear ridicule and coarse jests, freely bestowed upon those who dare assert that woman stands by the side of man—his equal."

And because they did not select those leaders, women had no real say in creating laws. Yet women were expected to obey the laws.

In the days following the convention, a number of newspapers and journals—all run by men—criticized the event. Women had no business voting, they said, and their demands for expanded rights were silly. But Mott, Stanton, and the meeting's other organizers were convinced it had been a success. "It will start women thinking, and men too," Stanton remarked. "And when men and women think about a new question, the first step in progress is taken." History would later show she was right.

THE MOVEMENT EXPANDS

CH. 2

*L*ucretia Mott, Elizabeth Cady Stanton, and the other

organizers of the Seneca Falls convention hoped they would see

female suffrage become a reality in their lifetimes. But it was not

to be. For American women, gaining voting rights lay many years

in the future. In fact, only one of the more than 200 women who

attended the 1848 meeting lived long enough to cast her vote. Her

name was Charlotte Woodward.

It is clear that Woodward would never have enjoyed that right

if not for the persistence of her sister suffragists. Not long after the

Seneca Falls gathering, women in New York and other states started

Charlotte Woodward had been only 19 years old at the time of the Seneca Falls convention in 1848.

holding many more such meetings. And they saw holding an annual national convention as a productive approach.

The first one took place in Worcester, Massachusetts, in 1850. The chief organizer was Paulina Wright Davis, a well-to-do Rhode Island woman. Because she was socially prominent, she encouraged participation by other high-placed women. Among them were noted social reformers Susan B. Anthony and Amelia Bloomer, although Anthony was not able to attend. Another was the country's first female ordained minister, Antoinette Brown.

The national meetings continued through the 1850s. But the pace of the blossoming women's movement suddenly changed in 1861.

That was the year the nation was first torn apart by the Civil War. Some suffragists felt they should continue their struggle. But a majority thought the war was so huge in scope that it overshadowed the efforts to obtain suffrage. It seemed more patriotic to funnel their energies into the war effort and resume the quest for civil rights when the conflict ended.

In the meantime, another civil rights struggle captured the attention of many women. The war's main cause was a difference of opinion over the expansion of slavery. Northerners opposed it, while most southerners supported it. When the conflict began, a number of Americans already belonged to the abolitionist movement, which sought to get rid of slavery altogether. Many suffragists came to sympathize with the plight of black slaves. They understood what it was like to be treated as social inferiors.

Several leaders in the women's movement reasoned that helping to abolish slavery now would aid their own cause later. Organizing against slavery, as some women had been doing for awhile, would give women in the suffrage movement needed practice for their own future organizing. As a result, thousands of American women became active abolitionists. They traveled through the northern states speaking out against slavery.

FORGING A NEW CHAIN?

When the war ended in 1865, some American women decided it was time to resume their struggle for suffrage and other rights. Their recent contributions to the war effort, including support for abolition, had greatly improved their image in the eyes of some men. President Abraham Lincoln seemed to speak for these men. "If all that has been said by orators and poets since the creation of the world in praise of women were applied to the women of America," he said, "it would not do them justice for their conduct during this war."

Many women were enthusiastic about gaining their rights as soon as possible. In the months following the war, leading suffragists were hopeful that Congress would soon address the issue. There was talk about amending the Constitution to give black people freedom and civil rights, including voting rights. It seemed only logical and fair that lawmakers would deal with the issue of women's suffrage at the same time.

Sojourner Truth was an abolitionist and women's rights activist.

But some women were worried that the all-male Congress might ignore their needs. African-American social reformer Sojourner Truth put this worry into words. "If colored men get their rights, and not colored women theirs," she said, "you see, the colored men will be masters over the women, and it will be just as bad as it was before."

Sure enough, when the 14th Amendment to the Constitution was ratified in 1868, it confirmed that black men were citizens. But no mention was made of women. Two years later the 15th Amendment guaranteed suffrage to all male citizens, no matter what color they were. Once more, however, women's rights were not addressed. And the states were still free to restrict women from voting. Upset over this turn of events, Stanton accused Congress, which had earlier passed the amendment, of forging "a new chain for our

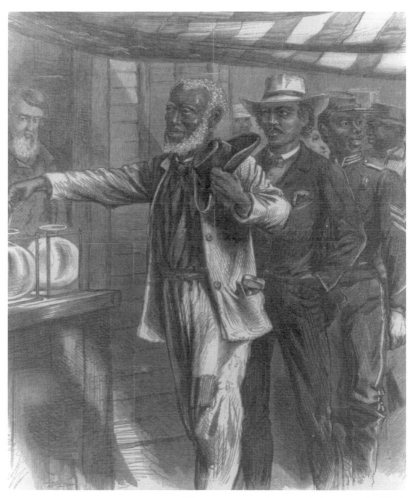

Black men were given the right to vote in 1870.

degradation." The lawmakers had not changed "the old idea that woman's divinely ordained position is at man's feet," she said, "and not on an even platform by his side."

A SPLIT IN THE RANKS

Stanton was not the only prominent woman who lashed out at what she saw as a betrayal of all American women. But as time went on, other women in the movement came to see that attitude as too bitter and angry. These moderates steadily broke away from those they viewed as extremists. Led by prominent suffragist Lucy Stone, in 1869 the moderates established the American Woman Suffrage Association (AWSA).

Lucy Stone was the first woman from Massachusetts to earn a college degree.

That same year Stanton and Susan B. Anthony founded a competing group. They called it the National Woman Suffrage Association (NWSA). This split in the women's movement set back all suffragists considerably. The rivalry between the two groups now absorbed too much time and energy. Not until they could patch up their differences and unite would the cause of women's suffrage have a chance for success.

THE MAIN GOAL IN SIGHT

CH. 3

*R*ivalries between women's groups did not prove

permanent. Leaders of the AWSA and NWSA came to realize

that their squabbles were hurting the cause. So in 1890 the two

organizations patched up their differences and merged. The new and

much stronger group was christened the National American Woman

Suffrage Association (NAWSA).

The leaders of the NAWSA set a daring major goal. It was to work

toward the passage of a constitutional amendment granting women

the right to vote. They were not the first to make such an attempt.

The National American Woman Suffrage Association was headquartered in New York City.

The NWSA, led by Susan B. Anthony, had gotten a women's suffrage amendment introduced into Congress in 1878. It had been soundly defeated.

But Anthony and her followers had managed to reintroduce the bill nearly every year thereafter. It came to bear the nickname of the "Susan B. Anthony Amendment." The newly formed NAWSA in a sense picked up where the NWSA had left off. Each year its members lobbied hard to get congressmen to take the idea of a women's suffrage amendment seriously.

Most of the top lawmakers in Washington, D.C., continued to oppose the amendment. Yet the suffragists met less resistance from some of the state legislatures, which they also lobbied hard. In the late 1800s and early 1900s, five western states—Colorado, Idaho,

Utah, Washington, and Wyoming—granted women the right to vote. More headway for the women's movement came in 1911 and 1912 when California, Kansas, Arizona, and Oregon passed women's suffrage bills.

Leading suffragists now felt that their main goal—giving all American women the right to vote—might well be in sight. They decided to increase their efforts to gain publicity. Any public activity that called attention to them and their cause seemed worth the effort. Some women learned to fly the new-fangled devices called airplanes, whose first several pilots had been men. Women also increased their participation in sports contests. Swimming

Women were given the right to vote in Wyoming in 1869.

competitions were particularly popular because the press was quick to cover and photograph women in bathing suits.

Suffragists also became adept at organizing parades, both large and small, and to celebrate almost any occasion. One of the biggest parades and most widely covered by the press took place in March 1913 in Washington, D.C. Successful lawyer and suffragist Inez Milholland led the way. Riding a magnificent white horse, she was followed by more than 5,000 women, nine marching bands, and many lavishly decorated floats.

Leaders of the NAWSA strongly urged women of all walks of life to attend the parade. Why? "Because this is the most conspicuous and important demonstration that has ever been attempted by suffragists in this country," said a letter to NAWSA members. "Because this parade will be taken to indicate the

Inez Milholland atop her horse at the Washington, D.C., parade

importance of the suffrage movement by the press of the country and the thousands of spectators from all over the United States."

WORLD WAR I

Such public spectacles did aid the suffragists' cause. Combined with behind-the-scenes lobbying efforts, they convinced more male state lawmakers to back women's suffrage bills. In 1914 such legislation passed in two more western states, Montana and Nevada.

The women's movement and its goals also gained attention through the actions of women during World War I. Although that immense conflict had started in Europe in 1914, the United States did not enter it until April 1917. Women across the country—suffragists included—offered to contribute to the war effort in any way they could. Some volunteered to work as nurses on or near the battlefields in France.

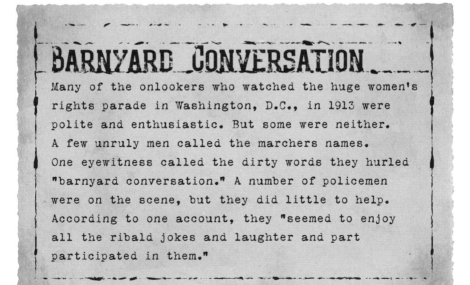

BARNYARD CONVERSATION

Many of the onlookers who watched the huge women's rights parade in Washington, D.C., in 1913 were polite and enthusiastic. But some were neither. A few unruly men called the marchers names. One eyewitness called the dirty words they hurled "barnyard conversation." A number of policemen were on the scene, but they did little to help. According to one account, they "seemed to enjoy all the ribald jokes and laughter and part participated in them."

Of those suffragists who remained in the United States, some organized war bond drives to raise money for the troops. Others rolled bandages for Army doctors and grew victory gardens to help feed themselves and take pressure off the public food supply. Still others took the places of men who were away fighting by laboring in munitions plants and other factories.

The hard work and sacrifices of millions of women during the war strongly affected attitudes about women's rights. Many American women who had not participated in the women's movement before the war now became suffragists. For example, late in 1917 the California State Federation of Women's Clubs publicly stated that denying women the right to vote on equal terms with men was an injustice. The federation urged Congress to enact an amendment to the U.S. Constitution giving women the right to vote. Women's contributions to the war effort also changed the minds of many men who had been against women's suffrage. They realized that women were just as patriotic as men and therefore deserved the right to vote.

ON A COLLISION COURSE

But there was still not enough support nationwide to pressure members of Congress into passing the 19th Amendment. This amendment intended to grant women the right to vote. So the women's movement pressed on with its campaign for the legislation. Carrie Chapman Catt, then in charge of the NAWSA, helped to organize peaceful protests all over the country.

Suffragists picket in front of the White House.

Meanwhile, a more militant offshoot of Catt's group, the National Woman's Party (NWP), turned to more controversial methods. Guided by Alice Paul, NWP members picketed the White House. In those days a majority of Americans saw this as a distasteful and overly aggressive act. When a reporter asked Paul why the NWP was doing it, she answered, "If a creditor stands before a man's house all day long, demanding payment of his bill, the man must either remove the creditor or pay the bill."

It was now clear that some women had decided they would no longer use polite means to get the rights they deserved. They had placed themselves on a collision course with the male authorities. People across the country waited to see what would happen next.

TRIUMPH OF THE HUMAN SPIRIT

*I*n the summer of 1917, newspapers across the country carried

articles about the suffragists picketing the White House. At first,

hoping to avoid giving the protesters the publicity they sought, the

police did nothing. Eventually, however, they started arresting the

picketers. The women initially received jail terms of a day or two. But

because they kept up their picketing, the sentences grew longer.

Finally the authorities decided to try ending the protests by

making an example of the ring leader. They arrested Alice Paul in

Women came out in support of Alice Paul after she was jailed.

October 1917 and sentenced her to seven months in a local jail.
Not long after they put her behind bars, she staged a hunger strike.
Paul later said it was the strongest weapon the suffragists had left to
carry on their battle. Paul's actions inspired other jailed suffragists,
who also refused to eat.

THE NIGHT OF TERROR

In the face of this show of courage, flustered and embarrassed
correctional officials made one blunder after another. First they
attempted to dishonor Paul by throwing her into a ward for inmates
needing psychiatric care. When this did not work, they placed
bright lights in her cell to keep her from sleeping. All the while she
still would not eat. So they held her down, brutally shoved a tube

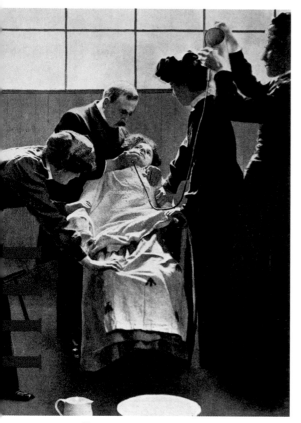

down her throat, and poured liquids into her stomach. This took place several times each day for weeks.

In spite of the awful tortures inflicted upon her, Alice Paul refused to give in. One of the doctors who examined her during her ordeal later commented that she displayed "a spirit like Joan of Arc, and it is useless to try to change it. She will die but she will never give up."

Suffragists in prison in England and the U.S. were sometimes force fed.

Meanwhile, many of the other jailed suffragists underwent violent forced feeding. Some had to ingest beans and cornmeal infested with worms. And officials would not allow several of the women any contact with their lawyers and relatives.

Unable to break the prisoners' spirit, the authorities moved the women to another jail and resorted to even crueler tactics. The evening of November 15, 1917, later became known as the "Night of Terror." The official in charge ordered between 40 and 50 guards to attack the women. Armed with clubs, the men pounded, slapped, choked, and kicked the prisoners, including a woman in her 70s.

Another women suffered a heart attack and was left to suffer on a concrete floor.

A prisoner identified as Mrs. Brannan later testified that the chief official, "directed the whole attack, inciting the guards to every brutality. The whole group of women were thrown, dragged, and hurled" out of one building and into another. There, "another group of bullies was waiting for us."

THE RIGHT SIDE OF HISTORY

The attempt to scare the suffragists into abandoning their demands backfired. Newspapers quickly found out what had happened, and the public was outraged. On learning how the imprisoned women had suffered, countless Americans changed their minds and began to support women's suffrage.

The support helped the NAWSA increase its pressure on both Congress and the president. Woodrow Willson had long opposed the idea of women voting. But now, with the tide of public sentiment flowing against him, he found himself on the wrong side of history. He could no longer ignore Inez Milholland's last public words before her unexpected death in 1916. "Mr. President," she had said, "how long must women wait for liberty?"

In January 1918 Wilson relented and agreed it was time for women to gain the right to vote. With his support, on May 21, 1919, the Susan B. Anthony Amendment passed the House of Representatives by a margin of 304 to 89 votes. The Senate dragged its feet for more than a year. But finally, on June 4, 1919, it passed

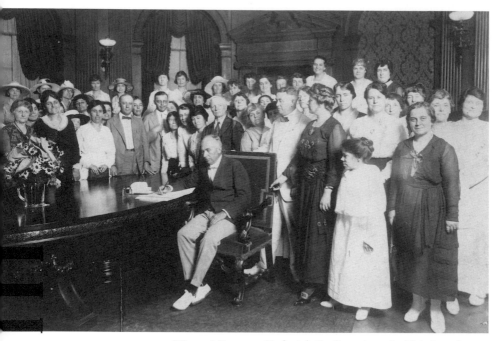

Missouri Governor Frederick Gardner signs the 19th Amendment, making Missouri the 11th state to approve it.

the amendment by a margin of 56 to 25 votes. The bill had to be ratified by 36 of the 48 states to become law. Tennessee became the deciding state August 24, 1920. Two days later the 19th Amendment officially became part of the U.S. Constitution. As a result, American women voted in a national election for the first time in November of that same year.

A TREMENDOUS DEBT

Seventy-two years elapsed from the Seneca Falls convention to the election of 1920. During that time tens of thousands of women had devoted part or all of their lives to the cause of women's suffrage. Without their dedication and hard work, women in the United States would not have won the right to vote.

Today many Americans take that right for granted. They might not realize the tremendous debt they owe to Mott, Stanton, Anthony, Paul, and the other suffragists. They not only secured the franchise for women. They also opened the way for women to gain other rights. Among them are holding public office, working in the military and other areas once open only to men, and receiving pay and education as men do. The suffragists committed themselves to increasing opportunities for women, no matter how long it took. It is perhaps not surprising, therefore, that their sacrifices and ultimate victory have often been called a true triumph of the human spirit.

Elizabeth Cady Stanton (seated) and Susan B. Anthony

INDEX

INTERNET SITES

Use FactHound to find Internet sites related to this book. All of the sites on FactHound have been researched by our staff.

Here's all you do:
Visit *www.facthound.com*
Type in this code: 9780756547356

GLOSSARY

ABOLITIONIST—a person who worked to end slavery

AMENDMENT—a formal change made to a law or legal document, such as the U.S. Constitution

AVERSION—hatred or loathing

CREDITOR—someone who lends someone money and expects to be paid back

FRANCHISE—the right to vote

INALIENABLE—undeniable

PICKET—to stand outside a place to spread your message

RATIFY—formally approve

RESILIENT—tough, durable, and hard to defeat

ROWDY—a troublemaker

SUFFRAGE—the right to vote

SUFFRAGIST—a supporter of women's right to vote

TIMELINE

1755–1769

The short life of the Republic of Corsica, the first modern nation to grant women the right to vote

1776–1807

The newly formed state of New Jersey allows women who own property to vote

1840

American social reformers Lucretia Mott and Elizabeth Cady Stanton meet while attending the World Anti-Slavery Convention

1848

Mott, Stanton, and a few other women organize the first regional U.S. women's rights convention in Seneca Falls, New York

1850

The first national women's rights convention is held in Worcester, Massachusetts

1911

Several state-level anti-suffrage groups merge to form the National Association Opposed to Woman Suffrage

1913

Suffragists stage an enormous parade in Washington, D.C.; more than 5,000 women march

1917

April: The U.S. enters World War I, and many suffragists begin contributing to the war effort

October: Noted suffragist Alice Paul is arrested and thrown into jail, where she is mistreated and brutally force-fed

November: Many suffragists are beaten, kicked, and choked by guards while imprisoned for picketing in front of the White House

The *New York Herald* severely criticizes the national women's rights convention held that year

1861–1865

Many suffragists learn to organize by joining abolitionist groups during the Civil War

1869

Suffragists establish two new women's rights groups—the American Woman Suffrage Association and the National Woman Suffrage Association

1878

Susan B. Anthony gets a women's suffrage constitutional amendment introduced to Congress; it fails to pass

1890

The AWSA and NWSA merge to form the National American Woman Suffrage Association

Wyoming joins the Union as the first state with voting rights for women

1918

On January 10 the U.S. House of Representatives passes the 19th Amendment

1919

On June 4 the U.S. Senate passes the 19th Amendment

1920

On April 26, after ratification by the states, the 19th Amendment is certified and officially becomes part of the U.S. Constitution

SELECT BIBLIOGRAPHY

Baker, Jean H. *Sisters: The Lives of America's Suffragists*. Hill and Wang: New York, 2005.

Camhi, Jane Jerome. *Women Against Women: American Anti-Suffragism, 1880–1920*. Brooklyn, N.Y.: Carlson Pub., 1994.

Cott, Nancy F., ed. *No Small Courage: A History of Women in the United States*. New York: Oxford University Press, 2000.

Evans, Sara M. *Born for Liberty: A History of Women in America*. New York: Free Press, 1989.

Felder, Deborah G. *A Century of Women. The Most Influential Events in Twentieth-Century Women's History*. Secaucus, N.J.: Carol Pub. Group, 1999.

Flexner, Eleanor, and Ellen Fitzpatrick. *Century of Struggle: The Woman's Rights Movement in the United States*. Cambridge, Mass.: Harvard University Press, 1996.

Frost, Elizabeth, and Kathryn Cullen-DuPont, eds. *Women's Suffrage in America: An Eyewitness History*. New York: Facts On File, 1992.

Goodier, Susan. *No Votes for Women: The New York State Anti-Suffrage Movement*. Urbana: University of Illinois Press, 2013.

Graham, Sara Hunter. *Woman Suffrage and the New Democracy*. New Haven, Conn.: Yale University Press, 1996.

Harper, Ida H. *The Life and Work of Susan B. Anthony*. Indianapolis and Kansas City: The Bowen-Merrill Co., 1899.

Hine, Darlene Clark, and Kathleen Thompson. *A Shining Thread of Hope: The History of Black Women in America*. New York: Broadway Books, 1998.

Kraditor, Aileen S. *The Ideas of the Woman Suffrage Movement: 1890–1920*. New York: Norton, 1981.

MacLean, Nancy, ed. *The American Women's Movement, 1945–2000: A Brief History with Documents*. Boston: Bedford/St. Martin's, 2009.

Mankiller, Wilma, et al, eds. *The Reader's Companion to U.S. Women's History*. Boston: Houghton Mifflin, 1998.

McMillen, Sally Gregory. *Seneca Falls and the Origins of the Women's Rights Movement*. New York: Oxford University Press, 2008.

Rosen, Ruth. *The World Split Open: How the Modern Women's Movement Changed America*. New York: Viking, 2000.

Rosenbloom, Nancy J. *Women in American History Since 1880, a Documentary Reader*. Malden, Mass.: Wiley-Blackwell, 2010.

Stanton, Elizabeth Cady, et al, eds. *The History of Woman Suffrage, Vol. 1*. New York: Fowler's and Wells, 1881.

Wellman, Judith. *The Road to Seneca Falls: Elizabeth Cady Stanton and the First Woman's Rights Convention*. Urbana: University of Illinois Press, 2004.

Wertheimer, Barbara M. *We Were There: The Story of Working Women in America*. New York: Pantheon Books, 1977.

Wright, Almroth E. *The Unexpurgated Case Against Woman Suffrage*. London: Constable and Co., 1913.

FURTHER READING

Hicks, Peter. *Documenting Women's Suffrage*. New York: Rosen Central, 2010.

Todd, Anne M. *Susan B. Anthony: Activist*. New York: Chelsea House Publishers, 2009.

Walton, Mary. *A Woman's Crusade: Alice Paul and the Battle for the Ballot*. New York: Macmillan, 2010.

The Split History of the

WOMEN'S SUFFRAGE MOVEMENT

ANTI-SUFFRAGISTS' PERSPECTIVE

BY DON NARDO

CONTENT CONSULTANT:
Zoe Burkholder, PhD
Assistant Professor, College of Education and Human Services
Montclair State University

COMPASS POINT BOOKS
a capstone imprint

About the Author:

Historian and award-winning author Don Nardo has written many books for young people about American history. Nardo lives with his wife, Christine, in Massachusetts.

Source Notes:

Suffragists' Perspective:

Page 4, line 3: Elizabeth Cady Stanton, et al, eds. *The History of Woman Suffrage, Vol. 1*. New York: Fowler's and Wells, 1881, p. 67.

Page 7, line 2: Carl Schurz. *The Reminiscences of Carl Schurz: 1852–1863*. New York: McClure, 1907, p. 14.

Page 7, line 17: Elizabeth Cady Stanton. *Eighty Years and More: Reminiscences, 1815–1897*. New York: Fisher Unwin, 1898, p. 148.

Page 9, line 10: "Address by Elizabeth Cady Stanton on Woman's Rights." Elizabeth Cady Stanton and Susan B. Anthony Papers Project. 18 Oct. 2013. http://ecssba.rutgers.edu/docs/ecswoman1.html

Page 9, line 17: Elizabeth Cady Stanton. "Declaration of Sentiments and Resolutions," Feminism and Women's Studies. 29 Oct. 2013. http://feminism.eserver.org/history/docs/seneca-falls.txt

Page 10, sidebar, line 6: "Address by Elizabeth Cady Stanton on Women's Rights." Elizabeth Cady Stanton and Susan B. Anthony Papers Project. 29 Oct. 2013. http//ecssba.rutgers.edu/docs/ecswoman1.html

Page 14, line 2: Barbara M. Wertheimer. *We Were There: The Story of Working Women in America*. New York: Pantheon, 1997, p. 143.

Page 14, line 20: Helen S. Peterson. *Sojourner Truth: Fearless Crusader*. Champaign, Ill.: Gerard, 1972, p. 67.

Page 15, line 8: Elizabeth Frost and Kathryn Cullen-Dupont, eds. *Women's Suffrage in America: An Eyewitness History*. New York: Facts On File, 1992, p. 202.

Page 20, line 11: "Marching for the Vote: Remembering the Woman Suffrage Parade of 1913." Library of Congress. 29 Oct. 2013. http://memory.loc.gov/ammem/awhhtml/aw01e.html

Page 21, sidebar, line 6: Ibid.

Page 23, line 6: Sara H. Graham. *Women Suffrage and the New Democracy*. New Haven, Conn.: Yale University Press, 1996, p. 106.

Page 26, line 11: "Happy Anniversary Nineteenth Amendment." Boston University Arts and Sciences. 29 Oct. 2013. www.bu.edu/wgs/news-events/

Page 27, line 4: Inez H. Gillmore. *The Story of the Women's Party*. New York: Harcourt, Brace, 1921, p. 274.

Page 27, line 18: "Profiles: Selected Leaders of the National Woman's Party: Inez Milholland." Library of Congress. 29 Oct. 2013. http://memory.loc.gov/ammem/collections/suffrage/nwp/profiles3.html

Page 29, sidebar, line 2: "Woodrow Wilson: An Address to the Senate, 30 Sept., 1918." 29 Oct. 2013. www.public.iastate.edu/~aslagell/SpCm416/Woodrow_Wilson_suff.html

Anti-Suffragists' Perspective:

Page 4, line 2: Elizabeth Cady Stanton, "Declaration of Sentiments and Resolutions." Feminism and Women's Studies. 29 Oct. 2013. http://feminism.eserver.org/history/docs/seneca-falls.txt

Page 8, line 7: "Suffragists: Heroes of the Civil Rights Movement." Awesome Stories. 29 Oct. 2013. www.awesomestories.com/history/womens-rights/declaration-of-sentiments

Page 8, line 14: *The History of Woman Suffrage, Vol. 1*, p.803

Page 8, line 19: Ibid.

Page 9, sidebar, line 3: History of Women's Suffrage: Women Out of Their Latitude. utc.iath.virginia.edu/abolitn/abwmbt.html

Page 12, line 2: Brenda Stalcup, ed. *The Women's Movement: Opposing Viewpoints*. San Diego: Greenhaven Press, 1996, p. 85.

Page 14, line 9: Gilbert Barnes and Dwight L. Dumond, eds. *The Letters of Theodore Weld, Angelina Grimke Weld and Sarah Grimke, 1822–1844, Vol. 1*. Gloucester, Mass.: Peter Smith, 1965, p. 430.

Page 14, line 22: Kate Millet. *Sexual Politics*. Urbana: University of Illinois Press, 2000, p. 69.

Page 17, line 6: Molly E. Seawell. *The Ladies' Battle*. New York: Macmillan, 1911, p. 119.

Page 18, sidebar, line 6: Ibid, pp. 75–76.

Page 22, line 4: "Pamphlet from the National Association Opposed to Woman Suffrage." Jewish Women's Archive. 29 Oct. 2013. http://jwa.org/teach/primarysources/orgrec_08_detail.html

Page 27, line 19: Almroth E. Wright. *The Unexpurgated Case Against Woman Suffrage*. New York. Paul B. Heber, 1913, p. 157.

Page 28, sidebar, line 5: *The Ladies' Battle*, pp. 75–76.

Page 28, line 6: "Woodrow Wilson: An Address to the Senate, 30 Sept., 1918." 29 Oct. 2013. www.public.iastate.edu/~aslagell/SpCm416/Woodrow_Wilson_suff.html

Table of Contents

A resident of Seneca Falls, New York—Elizabeth Cady Stanton—spoke some controversial words in July 1848. "The history of mankind," she declared, "is a history of repeated injuries and usurpations on the part of man toward woman, having in direct object the establishment of an absolute tyranny over her." Clearly she had chosen to mimic the U.S. Declaration of Independence. But instead of condemning the tyranny of the British king, she had women colonists denouncing the supposed tyranny of men over women.

CH.1

REVOLT IN SENECA FALLS

Stanton went on that "He," meaning men, "has never permitted her," meaning women, "to exercise her inalienable right to the elective franchise." That is, men had kept women from exercising the right to vote. "He has compelled her to submit to laws, in the formation of which she had no voice. He has withheld from her rights which are given to the most ignorant and degraded men — both natives and foreigners. Having deprived her of this first right of a citizen," the right to vote, "he has oppressed her on all sides."

Elizabeth Cady Stanton was an activist, editor, and writer.

Stanton titled her daring parody of the Declaration of Independence as the "Declaration of Sentiments and Resolutions." It became the official statement of a fateful public meeting she and her colleague, Lucretia Mott, had organized. It took place in Seneca Falls on July 19 and 20, 1848. Around 300 people attended

Lucretia Mott is protected from an angry mob that broke up a suffragist meeting.

and listened to speeches by Stanton and others. The goal of this convention was to stir up support for giving U.S. women expanded civil rights. It ended up marking the beginning of the nation's so-called women's movement.

THE WISDOM OF THE FOUNDERS

In their demand to be given voting rights, the Seneca Falls women went against political and social tradition. At no time in history had a major nation allowed female suffrage. There had been a few minor exceptions. The newly formed government of the Mediterranean island of Corsica gave local women the right to vote in 1755. But it was short-lived. France took over the island in 1769, and women there could no longer vote.

There was also the example of the state of New Jersey following the start of the American Revolution. In 1776 the state government allowed women who owned property to vote. But that liberty was removed in 1807. Thereafter the women of New Jersey and all other U.S. states abided by the wishes of the nation's founding fathers. In drafting the country's Constitution, they did not address the issue of who could or could not vote. They left it up to the states. And for a long time all the states, except for New Jersey in its 31-year span, saw fit to restrict suffrage to men.

Stanton and the other women who attended the Seneca Falls convention were not content with that state of affairs. They felt that it made women second-class citizens. In their view it was unfair that they could neither vote nor run for public office. That limited them

only to managing the home, raising children, and in some cases pursuing part- or full-time work outside the home.

TO RADICALLY CHANGE SOCIETY?

Most Americans—women and men alike—felt the Seneca Falls protesters' demands for expanded rights were out of line. Not surprisingly, therefore, in the days following the convention, a number of newspapers and journals were critical. The *Oneida Whig*, the leading newspaper in nearby Oneida, New York, asked, "Was there ever such a dreadful revolt?" It was "the most shocking and unnatural incident ever recorded in the history of womanity," the editors said. "If our ladies will insist on voting and legislating, where, gentlemen, will be our dinners?"

Another upstate New York paper, Albany's *Mechanic's Advocate*, took a similar position. Referring to the women's demands, the editorial stated, "It requires no argument to prove that this is all wrong. Every true hearted female will instantly feel that this is unwomanly."

If women were given civil rights similar to men's, wouldn't it make sense for men to suddenly begin doing some of the women's traditional duties? In such a case, the *Mechanic's Advocate* said, "the males must change their position in society to the same extent in an opposite direction, in order to enable them to discharge an equal share of the domestic duties" now done by women. The paper's editors rejected such a social reversal. "Society would have to be radically remodeled," they pointed out. Human social order had

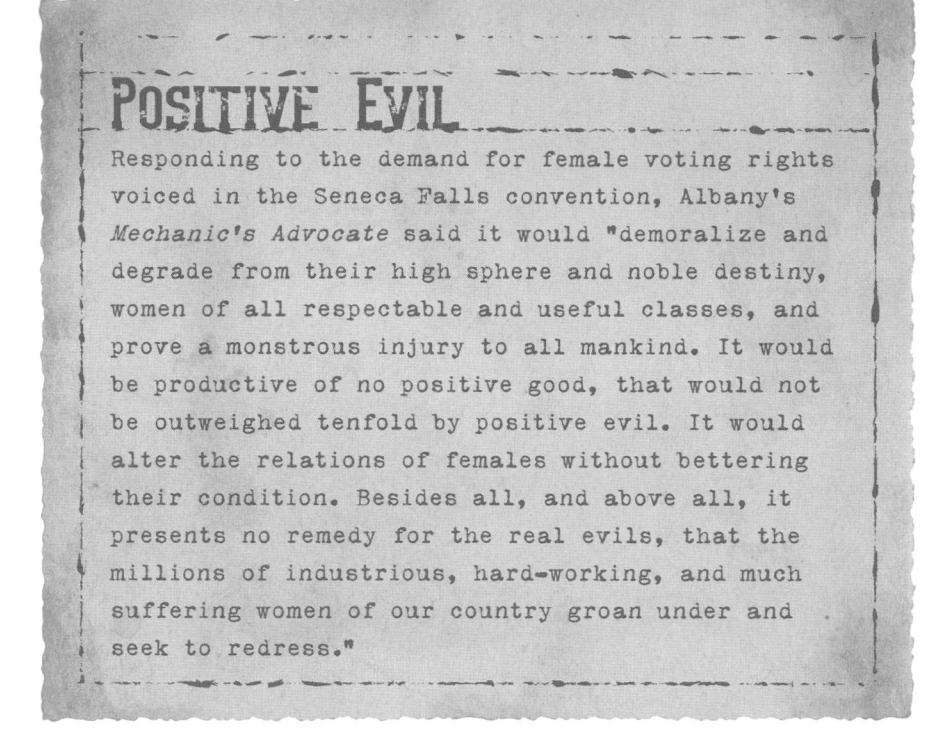

POSITIVE EVIL

Responding to the demand for female voting rights voiced in the Seneca Falls convention, Albany's *Mechanic's Advocate* said it would "demoralize and degrade from their high sphere and noble destiny, women of all respectable and useful classes, and prove a monstrous injury to all mankind. It would be productive of no positive good, that would not be outweighed tenfold by positive evil. It would alter the relations of females without bettering their condition. Besides all, and above all, it presents no remedy for the real evils, that the millions of industrious, hard-working, and much suffering women of our country groan under and seek to redress."

been rightfully "established at the creation of mankind." Her status had continued for "six thousand years." And the social order "would be completely broken up" if women could suddenly vote and hold public office.

In spite of these and other similar critiques, Stanton and her colleagues persisted. They continued to insist that women should be given civil equality with men. To press this demand, they organized more conventions. The women's movement slowly began to gain steam.

WHO IS TAKING CARE OF THE HOME

CH 2

hat do the leaders of the women's rights convention want?

That was the question the editor of the *New York Herald* asked in

September 1850. He was frustrated by the demands for civil rights

made by women in their frequent meetings. Only two years after

the 1848 Seneca Falls convention, the first national gathering of

suffragists had occurred in Worcester, Massachusetts. Because

the meetings and their demands were so unusual at the time,

newspapers big and small felt forced to respond.

The U.S. Senate only included men in 1850 and for many years to come.

The *Herald's* editor was no exception. He answered his own question about what female leaders wanted by saying, "They want to vote and hustle with the rowdies at the polls." In a mocking tone, he added, "They want to be members of Congress, and in the heat of debate subject themselves to coarse jests and indecent language."

Despite the criticism they faced, Elizabeth Cady Stanton, Lucretia Mott, and other suffragists continued pressing for the vote and other rights. One thing that irritated their opponents—men and women alike—was their apparent disdain for and neglect of their traditional female roles. Many average Americans wondered who was cleaning those women's houses and caring for their children while they were out protesting.

A large women's rights gathering held in New York City in 1853 left one local newspaper editor aghast. "We saw, in broad daylight," he wrote, hundreds of women shouting that "they should be allowed to step out of their appropriate sphere," the home, "and mingle in the busy walks of everyday life." The women, he pointed out, were obviously neglecting "those duties which both human and divine law have assigned to them."

Many men who read the editorial agreed with its author that the women were unattractive. Most of them were overly thin, he said. And they tended to choose new and daring clothing fashions that were indecent and tasteless. These included abandoning the traditional corset, which they said was too tight and restrictive, and even wearing pants like men! Such outfits, the editor thundered, made the women objects of disgust.

Most of all, however, the male critics made fun of the female protesters out of fear. But they rarely admitted it openly. Most upper and middle class men opposed women's attempts to gain the vote because they were worried about themselves. They reasoned that if women gained more rights, it would be harder for men to maintain their own social positions and authority.

THE SUFFRAGISTS IN WARTIME

During the Civil War, many American men found some relief from women's increasing demands for equality. When the war began in 1861, it quickly absorbed the time and energies of nearly all

Americans. Even many leading suffragists felt it would be both proper and patriotic to devote themselves to the war effort.

The women concluded that an important part of that effort concerned the status of the nation's enslaved people. Slavery was the conflict's central issue. Most northerners opposed the expansion of that institution, while a majority of southerners worried that the elimination of slavery would cause the South's economy to collapse.

Most suffragists sided with the northern position. By the thousands they joined the abolitionists, people who were fighting to get rid of slavery. It appears that these women identified with the slaves' predicament, feeling that they, too, had long been treated as social inferiors.

An 1864 Thomas Nast illustration depicted women in many roles.

But a few of the women were not content to dedicate all of their time to helping the slaves' plight. While speaking out against slavery, they also slipped in some of their own demands, including the right to vote. A number of male abolitionists found this troubling. They requested that the women refrain from complaining about their own problems. It was distracting too much from the abolitionists' main message, the men said.

The men were shocked when the women refused to stop advocating for their own cause. "If we surrender the right to speak in public this year," a suffragist stated, "we must surrender the right to petition next year." Women would next give up "the right to write the year after, and so on," she argued.

NO MENTION OF WOMEN

After the war ended in 1865, many suffragists looked forward to the upcoming 14th and 15th amendments to the Constitution. They were slated to confirm that African-Americans were free citizens with certain civil rights. The suffragists thought that the amendments might extend a number of civil rights to women as well.

But when the amendments were ratified in 1868 and 1870, they made no mention of women. Irate, leading suffragists asked if women were not citizens along with men. When one of Oregon's U.S. senators offered an answer to that question, droves of men across the country murmured agreement with him. "The woman who undertakes to put her sex in the adversary position to man,"

An 1870 collection of images celebrates the events leading to the passage of the 15th Amendment.

he said, "displays a spirit" that could potentially throw society "into a state of war, and make every home a hell on earth."

Some suffragists lashed out at the observation. But their anger backfired. Even many of their friends in the women's movement felt they sounded too shrill. So it was not long before the movement split, with two rival women's rights groups forming in 1869. The more moderate women joined the American Woman Suffrage Association (AWSA). More militant suffragists, such as Stanton and feisty reformer Susan B. Anthony, established the National Woman Suffrage Association (NWSA).

Activist Susan B. Anthony was also a teacher, journalist, and publisher.

Many American men were relieved. They saw that the two organizations poured much time and energy into competing with each other. For a while it appeared that the suffrage movement would steadily wane and finally disappear from the American scene.

VOICES OF ANTI-SUFFRAGE

CH.3

During the final decades of the 19th century, the suffragists proved to be stubborn. They refused to listen not only to men who opposed their views, but to women widely seen as reasonable. Molly E. Seawell was a prominent example. The socially conservative author of dozens of popular books, she argued that it was undignified for women to take part in politics. "It is my earnest hope," she declared, "that the sound good sense of American women will defend them from suffrage, and protect their property privileges," along with "their personal dignity."

Seawell added that women's chief duty was to raise sons who would be skilled at voting and running the government. With a great deal of sincerity, she told her fellow females, "I believe that the most important factors in the state are the wives and mothers who make of men good citizens to govern and protect the state."

Although they shouted down or simply ignored voices like Seawell's, the suffragists showed themselves to be incredibly resilient. Most people had expected their chief organizations, the AWSA and NWSA, to fade away. Yet over time the leaders of these groups saw the wisdom of joining forces. For what they viewed as the greater good, they merged in 1890 into a new and larger women's rights organization. Its commonly cited abbreviation, NAWSA, stood for the National American Woman Suffrage Association.

LACKING COURTESY AND DIGNITY

In her book *The Ladies' Battle*, anti-suffrage advocate Molly E. Seawell criticized the suffragists because they were impolite to President William Howard Taft when he addressed one of their meetings.

"The President spoke with the utmost courtesy and dignity," she wrote, "but on his making some guarded reference to the dangers attending the extension of the franchise, the suffragists proceeded to make history by hooting and hissing the President of the United States. This has never before occurred in the history of the country."

State presidents and officers of the National American Woman Suffrage Association gathered in 1892.

The women in charge of the NAWSA almost immediately set their sights on following in the footsteps of the NWSA's Susan B. Anthony. In 1878 she had managed to introduce into Congress a constitutional amendment that would have given women voting rights. The all-male members of Congress voted it down by a wide margin. It was no surprise. Almost everyone expected it to happen. Still the plucky Anthony refused to admit defeat and pushed for the amendment's reintroduction in Congress year after year. People came to call it the "Susan B. Anthony Amendment," quite a few of them sneering as they said it.

Mimicking Anthony the members of the newly formed NAWSA regularly tried to get congressmen to support the amendment. The women pointed out that some legislators on the state level were

leaning toward granting women the franchise. This turned out to be true. Beginning in the late 1800s and early 1900s, Idaho, Utah, Colorado, Wyoming, and Washington gave women the right to vote. A few years later Kansas, Arizona, California, and Oregon followed suit. This series of events gave the suffragists heart. More than ever they now believed that obtaining suffrage on the national level was within their reach.

RISE OF ANTI-SUFFRAGE GROUPS

Other Americans, however, were determined to make sure that women's rights to vote stayed well out of reach. Despite their rash of victories in the western states, the suffragists found themselves facing increased opposition. The voices of anti-suffrage were clearly on the rise.

Books and articles by Seawell, upper-class New Yorker Helen Kendrick Johnson, and other prominent women constituted only some of the voices. In the early years of the 20th century, many anti-women's suffrage groups formed. Several state groups merged in 1911 to form the National Association Opposed to Woman Suffrage (NAOWS). From its headquarters in New York City, it issued its central principle and goal. It was to educate the public that women could be more useful to the community without the ballot than if they were influenced by party politics.

The NAOWS and other anti-suffrage groups detailed many arguments they believed showed the folly of giving women voting rights.

One was that women who could vote and run for public office would abandon their families. Millions of children would then suffer from a loss of parental guidance. Also, a number of white southern men said they worried about allowing black women to vote. This would make it more difficult for southern whites to keep African-Americans in a subservient social position. Perhaps the loudest argument the anti-suffragists voiced was related to the sale of liquor. Many Americans worried that women armed with the vote would push for laws that made drinking alcohol illegal.

The National Association Opposed to Woman Suffrage was one of several groups opposed to giving women the right to vote.

RAISING EYEBROWS

To help advertise the arguments against allowing women to vote,

the NAOWS published and handed out millions of pamphlets.

One of the more popular stated that people should oppose women's

suffrage "because 90% of the women either do not want it, or do not

care; because it means competition of women with men instead of

co-operation." Also, "it is unwise to risk the good we already have

for the evil which may occur."

Some Reasons
Why We Oppose Votes for Women

Because the basis of government is force—its stability rests upon its physical power to enforce its laws; therefore it is inexpedient to give the vote to women. Immunity from service in executing the law would make most women irresponsible voters.

Because the suffrage is not a question of right or of justice, but of policy and expediency; and if there is no question of right or of justice, there is no case for woman suffrage.

BECAUSE IT IS THE DEMAND OF A MINORITY OF WOMEN, AND THE MAJORITY OF WOMEN PROTEST AGAINST IT.

Because it means simply doubling the vote, and especially the undesirable and corrupt vote of our large cities.

Because the great advance of women in the last century—moral, intellectual and economic—has been made without the vote; which goes to prove that it is not needed for their further advancement along the same lines.

Because women now stand outside of politics, and therefore are free to appeal to any party in matters of education, charity and reform.

Because the ballot has not proved a cure-all for existing evils with men, and we find no reason to assume that it would be more effectual with women.

Because the woman suffrage movement is a backward step in the progress of civilization, in that it seeks to efface natural differentiation of function, and to produce identity, instead of division of labor.

Because in Colorado after a test of seventeen years the results show no gain in public and political morals over male suffrage States, and the necessary increase in the cost of elections which is already a huge burden upon the taxpayer, is unjustified.

Because our present duties fill up the whole measure of our time and ability, and are such as none but ourselves can perform. Our appreciation of their importance requires us to protest against all efforts to infringe upon our rights by imposing upon us those obligations which cannot be separated from suffrage, but which, as we think, cannot be performed by us without the sacrifice of the highest interests of our families and of society.

Because it is our fathers, brothers, husbands and sons who represent us at the ballot-box. Our fathers and our brothers love us; our husbands are our choice, and one with us; our sons are what WE MAKE THEM. We are content that they represent US in the corn-field, on the battle-field, and at the ballot-box, and we THEM in the school-room, at the fireside, and at the cradle, believing our representation even at the ballot-box to be thus more full and impartial than it would be were the views of the few who wish suffrage adopted, contrary to the judgment of the many.

We do, therefore, respectfully protest against the proposed Amendment to establish "woman suffrage" in our State. We believe that political equality will deprive us of special privileges hitherto accorded to us by law.

Our association has been formed for the purpose of conducting a purely educational campaign. If you are in sympathy with this aim and believe as we do in the righteousness of our cause, will you not send your name to us and pass our appeal on to some one else?

NATIONAL ASSOCIATION OPPOSED TO WOMAN SUFFRAGE.

35 West 39th St., New York City.

The National Association Opposed to Woman Suffrage passed out millions of pamphlets supporting its members' beliefs.

The suffragists fought back against such attacks in part by organizing public spectacles that drew attention to their cause. For example, they organized swimming contests. It allowed them to appear in bathing suits that they knew would raise eyebrows. They also held parades, including an enormous one in Washington, D.C., in 1913.

The suffragists also cleverly improved their public image by taking part in patriotic activities during World War I. After the United States entered the conflict in 1917, suffragists worked as nurses and ran war bond drives to raise money for the troops. They also grew victory gardens to aid the war effort.

But the behavior of a minority of suffragists damaged the positive actions. Members of one women's rights group, the National Woman's Party (NWP), picketed the White House. Most Americans viewed it as highly offensive. So when the police began arresting these protesters, few people sympathized with the women or their cause. The women's movement again seemed on the verge of destroying itself.

THE DIRECTION OF HISTORY

$\mathcal{M}$any Americans were troubled to see members of the NWP

pressing their suffrage demands in front of the White House in the

summer of 1917. At first the authorities were lenient and ignored

them. But the women refused to back down from what most people

viewed as degrading activity. So the police felt there was no other

choice and arrested several of them.

What followed was a series of unfortunate incidents. The guards

in the jail where many of the women ended up should have treated

the prisoners with basic decency. But they did not. When the head

of the NWP, Alice Paul, began a hunger strike to protest her

A suffragist is arrested in 1917.

arrest, the guards overreacted. They force-fed her, causing her great discomfort. It only served to encourage other suffragists to follow her lead and reject food.

Even worse, the tenacity and courage the women displayed unnerved and angered the warden of the Occoquan Workhouse to which the women were taken from the jail. In the evening of November 15, 1917, he decided to teach them a hard lesson—he ordered dozens of guards to rough the women up. Several prisoners were injured and one woman had a heart attack that may have been caused by her terrified reaction to the commotion.

When newspapers reported what had happened in the prison, the American public was upset. Sympathy for the victims was so strong that some people who had been against women's suffrage changed their minds. Furthermore, the NWP, NAWSA, and other women's rights groups now had extra ammunition. They heaped more pressure than ever on individual congressmen and on the president.

Suffragist Lucy Burns formed the National Woman's Party with Alice Paul.

Getting President Woodrow Wilson to support the suffragists' cause proved a major turning point in their movement. Wilson had long been unsure that giving women voting rights was a good idea. But as time went on, more and more of his supporters urged him to support women's suffrage. He also recognized that women had contributed mightily to the war effort, and that gave them increased political leverage.

After weighing possible consequences, Wilson announced his support for women's voting rights on January 9, 1918.

Many Americans—men and women alike—were surprised and disturbed. They felt that he had given in too easily to people they viewed as social misfits. But for his own reasons, Wilson would not budge. In turn, his support for the suffragists gave political cover to several congressmen. They felt they could now back the Susan B. Anthony Amendment without being widely condemned. The next day, January 10, the House of Representatives passed the amendment. The historic vote was 274 for and 136 against.

STILL WAVERING

Meanwhile, the Senate was still not convinced. For many months its members argued among themselves, and several of them wavered back and forth. Some who were unsure consulted the speeches, articles, and books of social commentators and other experts. A majority of those individuals remained opposed to allowing women the franchise.

One of the experts was the widely read and respected British physician and social critic Almroth E. Wright. He argued that women were not intellectually or morally fit to vote. He said the suffragists made public displays of themselves because they were unhappy in their personal or work relationships. "The happy wife and mother is never passionately concerned about the suffrage," he stated. "It is always the woman who is galled [upset]" because she feels that men do not treat her as she would like to be treated.

But such arguments against women's suffrage fell increasingly on deaf ears. The tide of public opinion was flowing against them.

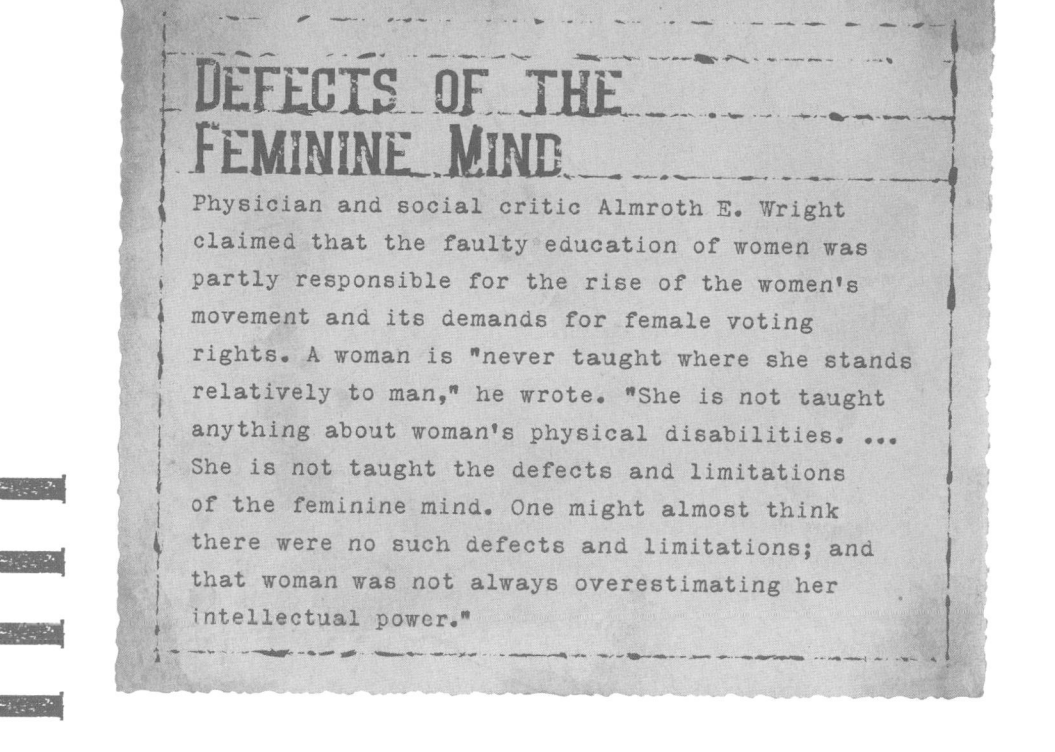

DEFECTS OF THE FEMININE MIND

Physician and social critic Almroth E. Wright claimed that the faulty education of women was partly responsible for the rise of the women's movement and its demands for female voting rights. A woman is "never taught where she stands relatively to man," he wrote. "She is not taught anything about woman's physical disabilities. ... She is not taught the defects and limitations of the feminine mind. One might almost think there were no such defects and limitations; and that woman was not always overestimating her intellectual power."

More and more women, and some men as well, came out for granting women the vote.

Witnessing the reality and recognizing the direction that history was going, President Wilson kept up his support. In an attempt to sway unconvinced senators, he addressed Congress on September 30, 1918. "We have made partners of the women in this war," he pointed out. "Shall we admit them only to a partnership of suffering and sacrifice and toil, and not to a partnership of privilege and right?"

LOGIC VS. EMOTION

Some senators who were against giving women the right to vote never changed their minds. But just enough did. The amendment passed the Senate on June 4, 1919, by a margin of 56 to 25 votes.

The bill then went to the states to be ratified by them. Ratification was certified August 26, 1920, making the 19th Amendment officially a part of the U.S. Constitution. Thereafter, women were allowed to vote in all national, state, and local elections. The only exception was black women living in the South, many of whom still could not vote because of racial discrimination. Many black men were not allowed to vote either.

As time went on, most women came to accept their right to vote without question. In their minds it seemed only reasonable that they should have the same rights as men. But some men disagreed. Even today there are men who feel that women are not their equals. They believe that men vote logically, whereas women allow their emotions to sway their voting choices. Clearly the issue of male-female equality has yet to be settled to everyone's satisfaction.

Suffragists, including Alice Paul (fourth from left), discuss ratification of the 19th Amendment.

INDEX